AF448606

SELF PUBLISHED @ZERO DOLLARS

LEAD YOURSELF TO THE FINISH LINE
THE MINDSET - THE STRATEGY - THE ENERGY

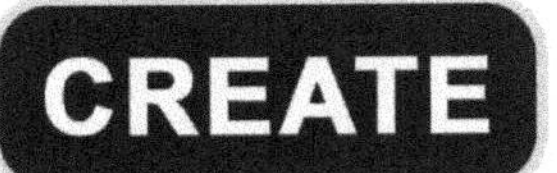

C. M. HOLLAND HZG

B"H

ISBN-13: 979-8-218-18876-4

PAPERBACK

NOTE FROM THE AUTHOR

Six months ago, I self-published a book titled SURF YOUR PIPE. It was an invitation to shift from 'stuck' to redeemed, leveraging strategies I had picked up along the way. I found that wherever I had been willing to step up my emotional maturity to consciously design a new way of perceiving a challenging situation, I found an element of personal redemption.

I used the metaphor of a surfer's mindfulness and focus, committed to an unpredictable wave, with its mastery unattainable by anything less than an actual flow state.

It reminded me of the radical presence needed to "surf my personal pipe," the daily, demanding, moving pieces of my life. (Dubbed Pipeline due to an underground construction site near the world-famous wave in North Shore, Oahu, Hawaii, the Billabong Banzai Pipe is one of the most dangerous and sought after wins in surfing.)

I felt called to share some of the breakthroughs I had undergone, hoping to ease the way for someone else.

When I heard about the innovative self-publishing option available for $0 (print-on-demand), it seemed like a lifeline, a way to share my story along with shortcuts and hacks to help the next person on their hero's journey.

I went all in.

I didn't waver.

I didn't look back.

I believed I could figure it out, and so I did.

I navigated any obstacles with an attitude of 'It's Gonna Work.' There was a runner's high when I hit the submit button, another when Amazon accepted it a few days later, and then again when over 100 copies of the book were sold in the first month. I celebrated when the first payment for book sales hit my bank account and every payment since!

As people started reading the book and sharing feedback, I was fascinated to hear just how many were quietly nursing the dream of writing a book.

Many shared how they had stacks of personal journals gathering dust in their garage or chapters of notes waiting on their phone and were just looking for the right moment to finish their book. And could I please help them self-publish?

(Even my therapist was ready to trade a session for self-publishing tips!)

TBH, I realized that my sweet spot was the writing, more than the technical part of self-publishing. So, I hoped that by sharing a basic run-through of my process, with the mindset, energy, and strategy behind it, I could help others feel confident enough to believe they could do it themselves, that being the most critical step.

And so here it is. Another handful of personal stories of where I was able to shift from a disempowered, victimized mindset to one of true freedom and empowerment (it's the journey of a lifetime), along with a run-through of how the actual self-publishing adventure went for me. It's all one and the same.

Our continued breakthroughs, micro-redemptions and inner work compound and expand our capacity exponentially, opening up more energy for us to co-create our reality and our legacy.

We may as well do it intentionally.

I just re-listened to the Self-Publishing course by Amanda Frances and Cara Alwill to birth this second book. May it be with a blessing.

B"H

TABLE OF CONTENTS
SELF-PUBLISHING INTRO

YOU CAN'T DO IT WRONG

SELF-PUBLISHING - THE BASICS

THE ACTUAL KDP RUN-THROUGH

WHAT NOT TO DO

THE FINISH LINE

NEVER WASTE A GOOD TRIGGER

THE GREAT COLLAB

TRUE FREEDOM

THE WISH LIST AND A STRAW HAT

SURF YOUR PIPE SQUARED

THE REAL QUESTIONS

SELF-PUBLISHING AFFIRMATIONS

CONCLUSION

FINAL THOUGHT

THANK YOU'S

TO MY CREATOR

SELF-PUBLISHING INTRO

"IF YOU CAN SEE IT IN YOUR MIND, YOU CAN HOLD IT IN YOUR HAND."

–BOB PROCTOR

You may be wondering if the title of this book is legit or just a gimmick. **SELF-PUBLISHED @Zero Dollars.** Can you *really* self-publish at no cost?

Great news.

The answer to that question is an absolute YES!

I'll walk you through it.

Well, here's the long and short of it.

While you absolutely can, it's like buying a car at the sticker price. Can you? Of course. Will you want to throw in a bit extra for seat warmers, the color you prefer, and an upgraded sound system (or whatever features you desire)? Most likely, you will.

Of course, you could manage without the "perks," but they add glam and ease to your life.

The same is true for your book.

You *can* have a generous friend edit it for free. (I went with the Grammarly app that my daughter uses to edit her high school essays).

You *can* download the PicMonkey or TextArt App and design your own cover. (Cara Alwil does that, and her 'basic' covers become beloved bestsellers.)

You *can* upload your manuscript to Amazon's KDP site at no cost. Yes, really. I did that.

You *can* also accept their free ISBN and Bar Code.

Finally, you *can* format the book, page by page, by following someone else's primary format. (I did that for my first book. It worked.)

This Self-Publishing companion aims to share some tips I discovered along the way and guide you around some of the pitfalls I encountered.

You will have the information to pick and choose where you'd like to uplevel professionally if and when that feels like a financial priority.

While information mastery, tools, and strategies are essential, the paradigm unfolding in the world is that your *emotional self-mastery* and energy will catapult your book over the finish line in a hyper-optimized way.

Sometimes, the most meaningful goals and achievements we desire are paused by everyday obstacles, inertia, or subconscious inner limiting beliefs. (Otherwise, we wouldn't be having this conversation). So, let's anchor in a trifecta of powerful tools by upgrading our mindset, strategy, and energy all in one fell swoop.

SELF-PUBLISHED @Zero Dollars

The Strategy

The Mindset

The Energy

You Can't Do It Wrong

There's a reason why your book is your book. It's your personal edge. Your fingerprint. Your story. **There's no way you can do it wrong.**

That concept felt like more than just a line in a masterclass about 'writing your big idea' and self-publishing. It felt like a profound truth of life.

Under the "guise" of a self-publishing course, Amanda Frances and Cara Alwill were creating art with their life experience, sharing values, concepts, and blueprints for your highest achievement, reminding me that it's all the same inner work.

Whatever you are doing, at this moment, in this lifetime, your authentic success comes from meeting up with your deepest self and connecting with your Creator/Higher Power. It's the *greatest love story ever* when you tap into your soul alignment and move forward from that headspace. Traversing the roadmap of life, wherever you come alive, is often 'trusty guidance' into your purpose.

The whole self-publishing course vibed like a welcome party for your soul, and a celebration of wisdom shared, friend to friend. It was an invitation to finally allow yourself to trust your intuition and innovate by creating a masterpiece that would be your addition to the world. Your mark on humanity. Your vision.

Life pressures us to follow the norms that others have

deemed the best or the only way of doing something, whether planning a career, having a family, building one's finances, or whatever applies to our lives. To succeed, we are subconsciously encouraged to doubt our individuality and trust society's path. Listening to 'outsiders' in place of our deepest calling trains us away from our internal guidance, dismissing our inner radar.

Amanda and Cara recommended starting our book wherever WE felt excited, expanded, lit up, and motivated. That would be the boss move with the most momentum-stacking impact.

And isn't that the truth about everything in life? If you crossed ten things off your to-do list but didn't make time for the one thing you *are* passionate about, you are left drained and uninspired. The day was lost on some level, along with continued access to your most authentic self. Likewise, when you prioritize the ONE thing that connects you to your higher purpose, all else falls gently by the wayside. (Well, for the most part!)

I loved the charge to follow our personal style in writing our book. To start wherever we felt called. Whatever got us moving. That was the key ingredient.

It was a homecoming to invite MY expression in, front and center.

It was a giving back of ME to ME. It was a sacred calling in of my message, a way to hear my inner voice. Me validating me. Me pre-approving me. I consult myself first, tuning out the chatter until I can identify my thoughts, feelings, and ideas. Once I can do that, embracing my inherent preciousness and spiritual self-expression, I'm genuinely ready to serve the world in an emotionally and spiritually healthy way.

For someone who had spent years becoming slowly invisible, dimming my light as the challenges of life bore upon me, this new paradigm was water on a parched soul, a celebration of coming back to life itself. An opportunity to set down any codependent traits and be there for me. An invitation to get reacquainted with my inner being and to find *me* from wherever I felt lost.

A reminder that I was worth my own time. That everything I needed at this moment was already inside of me and that intuiting my deepest soul desires was a gift of self-love and self-worth.

I started with an energetic declaration:

I desire to hold my newly printed, self-published book in my hand. I desire to be of high service to others. I hold the energy and belief that it all will come together in the most soul-aligned way possible for the greatest good of all. And so may it be.

B"H

Self-Publishing
The Basics

I saw a post scroll through my Facebook feed, authored by a guy named Matt Rud, describing his marketing process after he self-published. While he posted about his new book launch, he mentioned sitting at a cafe and ordering two lattes (I'm in already!). He said he sold 100 books right away from that coffee date with himself, logged in to his Facebook account.

I calibrated to how easy he made it sound.

The day my book went live on Amazon's KDP, I walked the two blocks to one of my favorite coffee shops and ordered an iced latte. (Just one, for me!)

I took a pic of my newly published book, *SURF YOUR PIPE,* and wrote a few celebratory posts. My emotions welled up. How had I made it to this day? I felt humbled, blessed, and in sync with my soul's alignment and life's purpose. It was a heady feeling. It felt like an auspicious, sacred moment in time. Everything else paled in comparison. I was on fire from the inside. Passionate about this creation and its delivery style of the messaging: demystifying the art of personal redemption.

Seventy-three books sold in the first ten days, with no other 'promo'.

Within the month, over 100 books were sold, thank G-d.

According to Matt Rud, once you sell the first hundred organically, with a minimalist launch, the algorithm adds distribution support.

It's intensely powerful how our belief systems drive our lives. I have also seen Facebook ads stating that most self-published authors only sell three to five books. Ever. What? Why would anyone stick around to listen to the rest of that scarcity-mindset belief system? They may sell you a winning product, but they lost my vote. I don't prefer to wire that belief in. I try to be intentional about what I listen to.

Amanda and Cara insisted that there was no reason we couldn't publish OURSELVES! They assured us that if we could write a social media post, we could write and self-publish a book. After all, it's just another medium for delivering content.

They shared the benefits of not working with a regular publisher:

More creative freedom, ownership of the rights, quicker publishing, choice in the book cover, and more money coming directly to you. Plus, you never have to pack and ship a book. Well, I calibrated to that belief and walked myself through the process.

I used to think of myself as tech-averse, so going to Bowker (myidentifier.com) to purchase an ISBN and a bar code made me sweat with resistance. I rhythmed my way forward, inch by inch, breathing through the process. Trust me, it wasn't just paying for a product with a cc. That would have been easy. You had to input a lot of info about your book. Title, Tagline, a short synopsis, publication price, and many other details. They even asked for my cover art; somehow, I managed to bypass that (whew!)

In other words, heads up. It's worth being prepared before you sit down at your laptop to create a Bowker login, assign an ISBN, and generate a bar code.

Amazon's KDP makes it *extra easy* to get an ISBN and bar code from them for free (it's SO tempting); it's just that then you can only sell through them. So, I took the extra step and got my own, but go with your flow and do what's best for you. Sometimes it's worth going with the easiest and most cost-effective option.

Let me pause here for a sec and share a profound lesson I learned regarding how hard or easy it would be to purchase and generate my own ISBN and bar code. I'm the queen of taking the path of least resistance whenever possible. I preserve my energy for the things that matter most to me, such as being there for my kids emotionally, driving them and their friends to and fro, writing, walking, praying, and listening to biz and self-growth masterclasses.

Anyplace I can find a shortcut to save time and energy, I'm there. (Ask anyone who knows me, I'm the queen of ordering takeout!)

When I sat down with James (graphic designer plus) at Starbucks on a late afternoon, midweek, to upload the book cover and spine that he had helped design and format for me, KDP's offer for a free ISBN was highly enticing. Even James was practically begging me to go with it. (It was a role reversal. He usually brought the energy of *let's do this right* for the long term. Now it was me pushing for the *longer, shorter path, which would take longer in the short term* but serve me better in the long term.)

It was a new mindset for me. I had heard Amanda Frances and Cara Alwil share that it was worth getting your own ISBN as it could ideally help with more potential options for long-term success. I found myself organically calibrating to their belief system. (Cheers to the superpower of good mentorship!)

At that moment, I transcended my nature and old patterning and held a non-negotiable energy that amazed even me!

I walked into Barnes and Noble yesterday and asked for their Self-Publishing section (not for the first time) and have been told that there still isn't any?! They didn't have even ONE self-publishing book for sale. What?! How is that even possible? It's 2023. There are *so* many people self-publishing and there are quite a few books for sale on Amazon about the relevant and trending topic of *how to self-publish.*

I'm guessing that many authors, self-published on Amazon, did not get their own ISBN and therefore couldn't get their books into some of the regular bookstores.

The employee was helpful and recommended that I

upload my book to Ingram Spark if I wanted to sell it to their bookstore. Some "smaller" bookstores don't appreciate how Amazon has changed the marketplace and don't prefer to order through them.

As I kept the momentum going on my self-publishing adventure, I tried to stay unattached to how each thing went, knowing that it was all an investment in eventually figuring it out. Any 'mistakes' would just be my wisdom going forward. All the while, I was expanding my capacity and stretching my window of tolerance to things on the edge of my bandwidth. My sense of self-worth grounded deeper, raising the bar on who I am and want to be. Someone who takes action on their vision and then leans back with trust. I was coaching myself through the process; one typed word in front of the other.

Matt Rud had another few insights. He proclaimed that a short, to-the-point book nowadays was a FEATURE. So much for the one-star reviewer who complained that my book was more like a pamphlet, not the size of a book. Hey, you can always check out the number of pages before you buy! At 137 pages, my first book was readable in one sitting. I was relieved and pleased to see that the anonymous book reviewer did not criticize my content, which is the most determining factor of any book. (This book, my friend, IS designed more like a pamphlet!)

According to Robert Holden, author of *Higher Purpose*, it's worth getting criticized when you are *in your purpose*. (The place where you feel alive.) He sees it as a chance to firm up his goals and objectives. Generally, someone with a genuine, intelligent critique and good intentions will stand behind their name. Rarely do people who are healed and whole, jeopardize their platform and name to damage another person's reputation and product.

In a 2-3 second micro-attention world, readers want a potent and inspiring message without the fluff. The bestselling books I have been gravitating towards these days are roughly 30 thousand words, 150 pages, and sized 5.5 x 8.5 inches, with a handful of pages left blank for the reader to pen notes as desired. (Just to give you a rough idea, this book is just over 14,000 words.)

Most everyone these days is saying that shorter is better. People want to get into a book, solve their problems (whether internal or external), and "get out." The reader, in essence, is paying for a connection to your energy and wisdom, aspiring to be transformed. Books truly are the most excellent investment and resource. They are an energetic exchange of a relatively small amount of money for vast knowledge and life experience.

(I personally savor the enjoyment of reading each book page and then rereading it! No rushing through for me.)

There's no wrong time to write your book.

You are the expert of your vision.

Sharing the gateway to your breakthrough is of high service to others.

I've heard a few authors say that their target audience is

the 5–10-year younger version of themselves. What they wish they knew then to have eased a shortcut along their path. To be honest, I'd say I wrote my first book for the current me. I find myself rereading it here and there to gain insight and remember the truth of who I am and my personal power to transform my journey by consciously choosing my thoughts, beliefs, energy, and actions.

B"H

The Actual KDP Run-Through

Logging on to KDP itself is exciting and gets your creative juices flowing, the page heading reading...

Create. Manage. Publish.

As you scroll through the setup, you will encounter the following actions to fill in:

Language: (choose your paperback's primary language)

Book Title

Subtitle

Series

Editions

Author

Contributors

Description

Publishing Rights

Keywords

Categories

Adult content: (yes or no, if inappropriate for children under 18)

ISBN: (Amazon's free one or your own at $150. If you go with your own, you can sell your book additionally through other stores)

Publication Date: I like to set myself a soft publication date to keep myself to a structured framework, along with a generous firmer later date. I personally choose an auspicious day as my goal.

Print Options: (Ink and paper type, trim size, bleed settings, cover finish- matte or glossy)

Manuscript: (upload PDF, DOC, or DOCX) KDP has not yet started offering the option of having them edit, format and work with your manuscript. I didn't spend money on editing or formatting. Instead, I paid a different price. I set my margins correctly for the right side of the book pages, but it didn't work out well for the pages on the left. The words came too close to the inner edge. This time, I'll prioritize a professional edit and format.

Update: I see multiple ads for companies adding support in book publishing. I can't tell if they are legit or not. Some are using parts of the Amazon Kindle name. Are knockoffs trying to capture a market without permission to work through KDP? I asked a small publisher not connected to Amazon, and he said that he thinks those guys are so small that it's not worth Amazon's time and money to sue them with a cease-and-desist order.

I further asked this one small publisher for his price points and options. For the least expensive package, you get royalties once a year. What?! You can't put a price tag on the magic when the payments for the book hit your account monthly, whether you sold a hundred books, a thousand books, or one book. The k-ching when you open your bank app and see a payment come in from a book sale is golden. It's strengthening.

Book Cover: People generally DO judge a book by its cover, so this is where it's worth paying a graphic designer a couple of hundred dollars to get your front and back cover just how you love it, as well as the spine of the book done clean and clear. KDP offers a calculator equation to figure out the size of your book spine based on the number of pages in your book. I ended up paying just over $500 for my first book cover (both sides and the spine).

This time I found a self-publishing company called (*Lee's Press and Publishing Company*) www.LeesPress.net that offered to create my entire cover, a la carte and do the formatting at an affordable price. I'm loving the way it's looking, and you can't beat their competitive price. For those who are banking on self-publishing at zero dollars, it's possible. You may just need a tech-savvy friend to help you with the sizing of the spine. KDP offers the info on how to figure it out and their rep will walk you through it.

Cara Alwil talks about using an app like PicMonkey to create your cover design. She is living proof that you can keep your covers simple and still be a bestseller. In general, the front cover aims to pique the reader's curiosity, while the back cover connects you to them by meeting them where they are.

When I went on PicMonkey, I had difficulty working with the images. (I think you do need some graphic sense to navigate it) However, the TEXT ART app I use for my Facebook and Instagram posts worked well to create a mock-up version of my cover page. BTW, **start** with your cover if it gets your excitement and motivation rolling.

I heard that KDP recently added the option of getting your book in Hardcover. They keep innovating and upgrading their options. (There's a reason Amazon is 'king'!)

Book Preview

Summary (ink and paper type, bleed settings, cover finish, trim size, page count)

SAVE AND CONTINUE

Territories

Primary Marketplace

Pricing Royalty and Distribution: While you can base your price point off of other similar books, at the end of the day, the buyer subconsciously 'feels' the energy of what you think about your price. If it's priced too low, you may feel resentful, and that frequency comes through. I've found that the best authors don't overprice their books, even though they could. They understand that the more affordable it is, the more people will purchase, which will bump up their rating and drive more sales.

SUBMIT And there, just like that, you've self-published your book!

25

YOU CAN CHANGE ANYTHING BY CHANGING THE ENERGY YOU BRING TO IT.

— **AMANDA FRANCES**

What Not to Do

The good news is that you can benefit from what didn't work out well for me.

While you can't do it wrong, as every 'misstep' and pitfall is wisdom going forward, here is what I now know for my second book:

I'm not gonna lie. Self-publishing is not for the faint of heart! (My daughter Kira would add that pretty much *all* of life is not for the faint of heart!) It takes drive, passion, a conscious intention, and a purposeful vision to **IMAGINE IT DONE.** It's doable. It just comes down to a series of small actionable steps that you need tackle only one at a time, with the mindset of **It's Gonna Work.**

I just ran into my friend Rivkie Feld at the coffee shop (where else?), and she asked if I could help her figure out how to self-publish her book, *The World Is in Lockdown, and You're Having Twins.* That was a couple of months ago.

We had a brief phone conversation, and when I ordered myself a BESTSELLER ENERGY mug off of Amanda Frances's website, I also got one for her, just to add to her high vibe on self-publishing. (Your frequency and vibration affect what you do and how hyper-optimized you do it.)

I understood that while she asked me for some tips, it was more the friendly moral support she sought. She texted last week. Her book is LIVE on Amazon. So excited for her. I ordered and read it in one sitting, astounded once again by just how POSSIBLE it is to take your words from heart and mind to paper and published. Her grit to land her book at the Self-Published Finish Line inspires me. She is a busy mom who kept moving forward on this dream without overthinking it. Like the four-minute mile, each time I hear about someone successfully self-publishing, it feels more and more doable for me, even for the second time around.

She mentioned that the few suggestions I gave her made a real difference. For example, I emphasized how I had not been careful enough to create wide margins, and the left pages in my book got swallowed into the gutter. As a result, she was able to save herself from that issue.

It had sounded so easy to make edits to the book once published. So, instead of waiting two weeks for a sample copy to proof what the printed book would look like, I pressed the SUBMIT button for the book to go LIVE on Amazon. It *took* a couple of calls to KDP to push the book through, followed by a sweet moment of joy when I saw it online. A deep soul shiver. A powerful moment stamped on my timeline of personal growth and celebration.

That momentum and energy kept compounding for the first five weeks, after which I went back in to upload some edits. There were a few typos and some sentences I wanted to add. Per my conversation with a KDP rep, their policy was that if the modifications were less than ten percent of the book, with the same cover, title, tagline, and author, they would approve the changes.

Well, it took over two months to get my few edits approved, which stalled some of my energy, as I didn't want to promote the book further at that point until the revisions were up and running.

What happened when they reviewed my edited manuscript, is that they went back in and started to give me a hard time about some of the technical elements of the cover, which they had *already* approved the first time around. What?! For example, they said that my bar code and part of the text on the back cover, as well as something on the front cover, were too close to the bleed line. It was a hassle and a half, as there ended up being so many layers to the graphics on the cover that it took time to work on that. And that was not even part of my actual edits.

Most books I've read, even with their professional edit, have a handful of small mistakes and typos.

So, I'd take the extra minute with your book to have it read through once more after the writing is completely done and before it's published, to check for errors.

And after that, I'd leave any typos alone because, guess what? After all that work and waiting, I'm left with a brand-new error that I didn't have before!

And this time, it stays! (For now)

STAY IN THE ENERGY OF THE END RESULT

The Finish Line

They tell a runner to focus on a point just past the finish line for the win, as it's a natural reflex to slow down once the goal is in sight.

Instead of just focusing on uploading my book to Amazon and Ingram Spark, I set my goal to get this book into Barnes and Noble to serve fellow readers at my favorite bookstore.

Nowadays, people are curious about self-publishing and want to hear from someone who has led themselves through the process in real-time so that they can attune to how it's done. We calibrate to each other's inspired creative vortex. We can put ourselves in environments as well as read books that help us dream bigger.

When we see that someone else has dared to show up for their dream, we believe we can as well.

A couple of years ago, I joined my daughter Sam (aka Tzipora) in an extreme sports activity, rappelling up "Wall Street" in Utah. It was a tall, rock-climbing mountain almost as flat as a wall. My daughter was belaying me that morning as I strapped on the harness to make my way up.

"On belay," said I.

"Belay on," said she.

"Climb on."

And up I went. After climbing about twelve or fifteen feet, I could not find a spot to put my right toe. I looked and looked and saw nothing but a tiny quarter-inch indentation in the stone that would never hold my weight. Worried, I looked down at the guide.

"Put your foot there," she insisted, indicating the small scratch in the wall I had already nixed. It didn't seem safe or doable.

The guide wisely shared that she had successfully climbed this mountain hundreds of times and KNEW that the small hollow (not more than a crack) in the mountain would do the trick. She gave me a minute to contemplate it and then offered me graciously and non-judgementally to come back down if that felt right.

From that twilight zone, hovering between trusting her experienced words vs. feeling limited and panicked by my outer circumstances, I closed my eyes. I *really* wanted to climb to the top. My desire was more potent than the familiar pull of the heaviness of life.

I took a breath and consciously decided inside of myself that I was willing to trust her words and believe I could do it. The power and impact of my intention brought on a frequency that propelled me to let go of my stable foothold and bring my right toe to the "nonexistent" indentation. I then used that momentum to scale the entire mountain relatively quickly, leveraging the energy that moved with me.

Everything has a wave and a frequency, self-publishing

included. We can set a goal for ourselves on paper, however, it's the emotional intelligence, personal growth, mindset, and energy that pull us into the flow of creation. The more meaning we infuse into our vision, the more we can collapse time towards reaching our goal. It's our personal energetic signature.

The energy with which we do a thing determines the outcome of that thing.

It's how John U. Bacon led the (Huron) "worst" hockey team to success. Besides hard work and excellent team spirit, he trusted fully in them, which activated their belief in themselves. He created an energy of self-leadership.

"Thinking is potent." (Likutei Dibburim Vol.1 Ch.1 pg.1 An Anthology of Talks by Rabbi Yosef Yitzchak Schneersohn)

It all starts with a thought which knows no bounds. It's the forerunner of all of our behaviors.

Focusing on a desired thought leads us to make a conscious decision, which propels us to take inspired action.

I saw it with one of my daughter's desires to go to a particular school. She felt called to go there. It wasn't affordable in any way, shape or form. As her mom, I knew that attending that school would angle my daughter for success spiritually, emotionally, academically, and socially. Something rose deep and fierce inside of me. I heard myself agree to take responsibility for the plan. (It was almost like an out-of-body moment.)

I prayed with heartfelt tears. I asked to be Divinely guided. I filled out many scholarship forms and much paperwork. I uploaded bank statements and taxes. I listed sibling info and expenses.

I refused to entertain any (well-meaning) naysayer energy that came my way, of why it wouldn't realistically work.

My daughter was accepted and thrived. She won the class award at the end of the first year. She made friends with the students and developed a great connection with her teachers. Her principal matched my energy and supported her growth and development in an unprecedented way.

She was accepted to the top three college/seminary programs of her choice. She chose the one where she would grow the most emotionally, spiritually, and academically. The "unrealistic" energy that went into this dream reaped "unrealistic" results. I love how Amanda Frances refers to herself as an unrealistic goal achiever. I'll calibrate to that thought any day!

What better evidence of the power and impact of our mindset, energy, and strategy?

When we change our energy, we change our life.

We realize it's just an illusion to think we can only be happy when something outside of us happens.

Nothing can stand in our way when we connect our minds and heart toward a vision greater than ourselves.

B"H

Never Waste a Good Trigger!

I'm not sure how my driver missed the turn-off. I had seen the ONSITE sign out of the corner of my eye. TRUST THE PROCESS, the words whispered. So, as the taxi circled back around the road, I tried to relax the frustrated knot in my stomach, knowing that my perfectly planned timing to make it to the welcome session had been for naught.

Perfection being overrated, I decided to let it go.

So fundamental and yet game-changing how our energy can completely shift in a heartbeat when we surrender to the unfolding journey. As per Joe Dispenza's refrain, "when we change our energy, we change our life." If the program's motto was to trust the process, who was I to stress over the timing of my arrival?

As I slid onto a cushioned bench in the back of the luxe, cabin-style room, eager and expectant faces greeted me briefly. I could feel the tangible hopefulness in the air, delicately intertwined with an element of anxiety as to whether this investment of time and money would pay off. Most participants had a lot riding on this Healing Trauma workshop. By the time they had found their way there, their spouse had either left them or was headed out the door; or possibly, their trauma symptoms had gotten in the way of completing their college degree or showing up for their job. It was serious.

Honestly, I don't know anyone who wouldn't meet criteria to benefit from that course!

Brows were furrowed. Expectations were high. Some people felt awkward and uncomfortable, worried that they may be unable to muster up the courage to look at the wounds that had brought them in the door.

The apprehension in the room was palpable. Hence, the meet-and-greet activities were meant to warm up the crowd and put everyone at ease.

I'm not a fan of icebreakers. To me, they feel shallow and silly, such as when someone gives a directive,

"Anyone here from the West Coast, stand on this side of the room…from the East Coast, stand on that side of the room." They were trying to find ways of showing common ground. That doesn't do it for me.

That being said, one way they grouped us at the end of that activity resonated. They asked everyone there for the first time to stand on one side of the room. Most of the participants shuffled over. There were about ten of us left. Then they called out to everyone there for a second time, and so on. One by one, the crowd kept moving until there was just me and one fellow left. It was my fifth time there. I felt like a kid in the candy shop. Excited. Eager. Hopeful. Joyous.

I had been there four times, so I KNEW in my gut that there

was NO WAY someone who showed up wouldn't get a massive shift. It might look different than expected, but everyone would get their money's worth and their most precious currency's worth, their time. (I'd bet my bottom dollar that even the one woman I ever heard stand up at the closing ceremony, rigidly insisting that the program didn't work for her, will get home, and be called to admit that she did get a shift after all.)

Even someone who felt timid or uncomfortable at the thought of participating in psychodrama work could still benefit from a wealth of personal growth just by being part of their group's energy.

There are many ways to do the inner work. Stamping trauma on paper, by writing and drawing your ten most significant life events (on a timeline) and then sharing them is one way. It can be a foot in the door to experientially look at the pieces of one's life story and see where distorted belief systems took hold, leading to "adaptive" behaviors.

The possibilities of processing and releasing trauma are as infinite as ways of being traumatized. The sacred work connects our finite selves with the part of us beyond ourselves, creating unity within our diverse and fragmented parts.

I may have been the only person in the room with off-the-charts excitement and not nervous or worried about the outcome. Even so, one guy was raising the bar for me. This was his seventh time here. My hero. If he could do it,

I could do it. (And so, Onsite keeps its spot in my vision-board-journal.)

I love that exquisite energy shift that happens when day three slides around. The tense energy dissipates as unmet childhood emotional needs are finally given a safe space to be addressed. Faces are altered. Creases around the eyes soften. After years of worry and resistance to facing fears, I wouldn't be surprised if phone facial recognition gets affected. That's how powerful and profound the healing work goes.

The facilitators wisely take their time setting up emotional safety in the groups. On Day 2, the type-A individuals are usually frustrated, skeptical of the process, and worried that things aren't moving fast enough. They don't yet have a way of appreciating that the deeper the foundation of emotional safety gets set, the deeper the work can go.

Each time I pull up at the beautiful, green campus, I get the embodied sense that I'm HOME. It's my happy place. Everyone is treated with sacred respect. People show up with the ultimate goal of becoming more of whom they already are —clearing the blocks/wounds that need acknowledgment and love as they face unspeakable trauma endured and bear their unbearable grief. It's an emotional intimacy with one's essence that rejuvenates and recharges, bringing on a sense of freedom that thus far was just a cellular memory.

As part of the workshop's policy and protocol, participants are discouraged from sharing their profession with anyone.

It's grounding to get to know people without preconceived notions. In this day and age, to be defined by something other than your work is cutting-edge.

Here or there, though, it leaks out. For example, the clinical director for this particular weekend mentioned a music event she attended in Boston with close to 500,000 people. "It was 250,000 people," a voice in the room called out. "I produced that event."

In the last few hours, just before the program officially closes, the friends you made morph into gossip columnists, professional singers, documentary producers, homemakers, world-class heart surgeons, construction workers, linguists, authors, coaches, and teachers etc. before your very eyes, as the veil is lifted, and social media contacts are exchanged.

While in this program, I felt like a student attending the college of her dreams. The emotional work available was a true art form. The masterful facilitators, who had done much of their inner healing work, were humble, sharing candidly that they were just one step further along their path than we were. Their inquiries were made with reverent respect. They leaned gingerly into our emotional well-being:

Would it be okay if I shared some feedback?

Are you open to trying this approach?

What's coming up for you?

Are you willing and able to show up for your group members

right now?

Do you need anything around this?

Is this a good place to stop your work for now?

If I could pay for a room on the campus as a timeshare and live there on and off throughout the year, attending the workshops on an as-needed basis, that would be #goals for me!

I watched and waited. As the six members in my group did their big "piece of work," I was curious about what would come up for me and how that would look. I was completely open to the possibilities. I wondered just where my veil of consciousness would be lifted.

When the hot seat fell on me, I opened with the fact that my daughter Mia had passed away about ten months prior, and I knew that I had barely accessed my grief, for understandable reasons.

Firstly, I had to be ON for my kids at home. I couldn't afford to fall apart or miss a beat on the carpool, school homework, hip-hop dance class run, or any of the daily routines. The kids needed stability.

On a deep level, *I knew better than that.*

I understood that if I modeled *not attending to my grief,* I was teaching my kids that it was okay to suppress their feelings. That's not what I wanted to show them. However, after years of my daughter's prolonged suffering and after experiencing traumatic grief over her near-death experiences, medical issues, and constant surgical procedures with their aftermaths, I was numb. Her actual passing seemed surreal.

I resonate with Melanie Tonia Evan's theory. Where my energy goes is where my kids' energy goes…

I knew the most impactful thing I could do to support my kids emotionally was to take care of my emotional health. Hence, the extraordinary energy I put into getting to this healing trauma workshop.

On a quantum level, as Joe Dispenza teaches, we cellularly help those around us shift as we shift. Our DNA and biological systems are interconnected, so I was hopeful that my inner work would add strength and healing to the family, as we are each other's mirrors.

Throughout the Trauma Healing course that week, I became more aware of how trauma immobilizes us, especially when it has been relentless. We lose our consent, our ability to have a voice. Traumatic grief is another whole level of pain. (Prolonged suffering, a sudden, shocking event) I hadn't known there was a difference.

When a slide was projected onto a screen with the word TRAUMA circled in the center and about twenty-five symptoms of trauma written around it, it was a lightbulb moment. I more clearly saw how my family and I were surviving life through the lens of the trauma we had experienced. We had some connection to almost every symptom on the page.

That explained my recent *insomnia,* which had never been an issue before. My *apathy* made sense as well. I spotted *risk-taking* as a trauma symptom. So maybe that was why my daughter Sam's motorcycle stunt-riding took off shortly after Mia passed. It all made sense in context. That bears repeating. Look at your life, your behaviors, and those of the people around you.

IT ALL MAKES SENSE IN CONTEXT.

At the end of the day, we can only be as emotionally available to the people in our lives as we are to ourselves. I thought I had been present for my kids all the years, and I know I was on some level. It turns out, though, that to the extent that I was in a trauma bond, self-medicating with my mocha lattes and pastries (my love language!) just to stay steady, I was barely emotionally available to tend to my own wounds. So, not as ideal of a mom to my kids as I would have wanted to be. Not for lack of trying and caring. I gave 100 percent of whatever I *did have* to offer.

Nowadays, you're practically an outlier if you are not healing from trauma!

Per the.holistic.psychologist Dr. Nicole LePera's Instagram posts, my emotional development may be at less than an 18 year old if I'm impulsive, entitled, take everything personally, believe I'm responsible for how others feel, and if my sense of self comes from outside approval. (Exhibit A here! Well, that *used* to be me.) At this point, I understand that my self-worth and identity come from within.

In general, we live in a grief-avoidant culture, so on the daily, no one even mentioned my daughter Mia's name to me. I get it. People feel uncomfortable and don't want to say the wrong thing. At least at home, the kids and I were organically weaving Mia's name into our conversations to keep it real. Otherwise, I may have been inclined to head to the hospital parking lot, take the elevator to the pediatric unit on the fourth floor, and check if Mia was still there!

I loved how the morning lecturer talked the talk that week. In a raw and vulnerable way, she shared her journey without judgment, shame, or resentment. Instead, she sprinkled gratitude towards the people who had shown up for her, inviting her personal growth, whether through kindness or triggering behaviors.

"Never waste a good trigger!" She would encourage us with a lilt in her laugh.

I took notes furiously, unlike my previous four times there. I didn't want to forget any valuable messages, and now my journaling has become precious content for authoring books. I want to be of service to the majority of the world that doesn't know that this type of emotional work is available, doesn't yet understand its strong value, or cannot afford it.

Why not share a taste of the magic and support?

Back to my moment in time. Cumberland Furnace, Tennessee. Onsite. Sitting in the soft, cushioned yet sturdy, chair. Seven sets of eyes on me. I needed to figure out where to access the dark night of my soul. And which one?

The facilitator, exuding enough calm energy to hold the context of emotional safety and healing for likely the whole country at that moment, talked to my soul.

Are you willing to try something, Chaya?

Willing, I was.

After all, they didn't set up all of that emotional safety for nothing!

She asked me a few thin questions about how sitting Shiva works in the Jewish community. At that point, I allowed myself to trust her and be led on a journey. The small room morphed into a shiva home. A chair was placed in front of me, slightly to the right. A comfortable distance. Just close enough. One by one, the six friends in the group took a seat. They looked me tenderly in the eye and offered their condolences. Each one freestyling their personal self-expression, sharing a word or thought of comfort, talking genuinely and softly to my essence. They showed up with presence, inviting me gingerly to show up fully as well.

The emotion started to well. Tears sprung up.

My heart ached.

I let my pretenses down.

I allowed my grief to be exposed.

I felt the love. I took it in.

I felt transported back to that actual first week after the funeral.

It was a journey beyond definition.

When Mia passed away, I operated in "function" mode. The funeral arrangements, the kids, the food, the chairs needed for guests, etc. I was the point person for all of it.

Not only that, just days before, a large check that I had been expecting and counting on was flagged as fraud, and the bank froze my account. As a result, all three of the tuition checks I had written to my kids' schools weren't going to clear, nor would the autopay for many other bills go through. It was unnerving at a time when I was already destabilized, and yet there was nothing to be done but let it go.

I couldn't afford to un-numb my feelings and likely wasn't able to access them even if I had the space to. So, while I greatly appreciated the kindness of each person who showed up to add support and comfort (may they be abundantly blessed), most of it had no place yet to land.

Almost a year later, I surrendered, away from my usual responsibilities at home, with my phone off, in a roomful of souls that had modeled courage to show up and face whatever was emotionally terrifying for them to look at and feel. I felt the grief. I allowed myself to cry unabashedly. I could hardly breathe. My ego's status was relegated to persona-non-grata.

The group facilitator took the seat last. She just sat there.

She didn't offer a word. Her condolence was above language. She held space for the both of us.

I viscerally felt Mia's presence hovering. It's said that during the week of sitting shiva, with the community sharing positive memories, it's as comforting and essential for the ones who pass on as the ones who live. The deceased draw joy from being remembered, acknowledged, and loved as their soul is pulling away from its attachment to this world. I *know* that Mia was there at the makeshift shiva. I felt her being comforted and finding another level of peace.

I had gotten what I came for.

Those ten metaphysical minutes were the reason for everything that had led up to sitting in that chair:

The months of vision-boarding my desire to go to Onsite.

The willingness to pause the outdated narrative of my life.

The facing of my plateaued emotional maturity.

The funding arrangements.

The flight.

The taxi.

The roommates.

The meals.

The group lectures.

The profound awareness of how trauma affects us.

The agreement to put down my phone for a couple of days.

The participation in establishing emotional safety in the room.

The deep listening as the members of my group shared their raw pain.

The prioritizing of this rich emotional work.

The willingness to tend to my thoughts and feelings.

The expanded capacity to hold space for my personal growth.

The flexibility to try something new.

The moxie to participate in psychodrama work.

The deep surrender.

The emotional trust fall.

The galactic meeting of finite and infinite.

Each step compounded the energy of showing up for my deepest self. By the time I sat in that chair for a "second" shiva, the healing manifested in a hyper-optimized, exponential way, collapsing time, space, and in this case, worlds.

NOTE TO SELF- TRUST THE DIVINE PROCESS

49

IF YOU WANT TO BRING HEALING THE THE WORLD, YOU MUST HEAL YOURSELF FIRST

-ELIMELECH OF LIZHENSK

B"H

The Great Collab

Head's up

I wrote this chapter BEFORE there was any collab.

I sat at my round, wooden Crate and Barrel table and dared to imagine the quantum leap I desired in my business.

There was a campaign that I wanted to work with. The movement had started with some friends actively beginning to use the phrase **Thank You, Hashem** (G-d). The organization's name embodied an expression of gratitude to G-d. It was a living prayer. A blessing. An acknowledgment of G-d's goodness and kindness.

A song was written with those three words. It was first sung at a joyous family occasion. Then, Joey Newcomb, a singer about to release a new album, heard it and asked to add the song.

It became a hit right out of the gate. A phenomenon. A powerful sound bite. A wake-up call. People felt called to express their connection to their Creator with love and thanks. From preschoolers to grandparents, its catchy energy spanned a global gamut. The yellow merch was on car bumpers, sweat jackets, phone cases, etc. Any money that came in from swag went right back into funding more of the same, as well as projects to help different groups in various ways.

It was messaging that I took personally. My kids had

picked up that soul expression from me, and I'd hear them remark, "thank You, Hashem," when something went their way. I desired to deepen my connection with my Creator, and continually show appreciation and gratitude for the myriad of blessings in my life. Juggling many challenges, nothing less than a perpetual *living state of gratitude* to G-d was cutting it. It became a significant part of my life's context.

In the original SURF YOUR PIPE manuscript, I mention my belief that no one can harm us or help us unless it's part of our Divine journey. To the extent that we surrender to how our life plays out, trusting in G-d's ultimate plan for our personal growth is the extent that we embody our soul alignment. The truth of who we are. When I realize that all anyone can ever show up as on my journey is a messenger of wherever I need to firm up my sense of self, I shift out of blame and into **gratitude.** I take full responsibility for my inner being.

The mini-tambourine keychain I was producing would be a great fit for the #tyH (Thank You Hashem) brand. I envisioned the collab going viral, sticky, and contagious with the messaging of **personal redemption** flowing from **gratitude**, the "shortcut" into our essence, our deepest selves.

I imagined every woman and child sporting a mini-tambourine keychain with the #tYH logo. It would hang from keyrings, backpacks, and handbags. Its picture would find its way onto the cover of Forbes, O, Entrepreneur start-ups, and many other publications, integrating body and soul on another level, the authentic keychain being a trendy and beautiful energetic symbol of redemption.

* (Throwback to Miriam the Prophetess, from Biblical times, who fashioned tambourines with her sisters during the darkest of times to wake up their yearning for and belief in their redemption from the Egyptian exile. Their anticipation and longing for freedom activated an energy inside of themselves that drew it towards them.)

It was a humbling thought that something as small and seemingly inconsequential as a keychain could be a vehicle to spread an energy of gratitude to G-d. A vessel. A chariot. A facilitator. A catalyst. A spark. A driver. A carrier. A container. A receptacle.

Update as I write this book:

A first order is in for 100 pcs!

#Thank You, Hashem (G-d) #tyhnation.com

The first order feels like zero to one, the breakthrough step.

May it be with an exponential blessing!

Update as I edit this chapter:

The mini tambourine keychains with the #tYH logo came out beautiful. The color we chose for the wood to match the logo hit perfectly. They are currently on sale on the #Thank You Hashem website, showing up under the 'Nashim Tzidkanios' category, when you scroll through their merch.

I am feeling blessed and thankful. Grateful for evidence of how what is meant for us aligns relatively easily, when we let go of the attachment to the outcome. I know that when one door closes (something that's not aligned with my life's purpose), another will surely open, so what is there really to worry about on my divine journey. I do my part and trust that G-d has my back.

True Freedom

I've managed to avoid addressing some of my poorer habits for many years. "It's ok," I would tell myself. "I'm doing great for living in survival mode." And that HAS been true. And now, (drum roll, please...) with compassion, grace, and self-love, I'm ready to raise the bar.

That's a formal declaration to G-d's universe. I, C. M. Holland, am ready to step into a deeper version of my truth. I desire to heal for real. I'm willing to part with some areas of self-sabotage. Not from a place of guilt or force (that would be disempowering) but from a place of love and gratitude for how far I have already come.

Where to start?!

I knew that anywhere I could liberate some emotional energy by processing any guilt, shame, fear, or regret that I might carry could free space up for more personal and professional growth and expansion. However, I also knew that essential self-care was a sore point for me, having become so used to putting everyone else first (caretaker fatigue), which had led to the pause on some of my vision.

I studied the quantum leap result equation, looking for the ideal spot to access the next-level ME. The place where I currently felt called to show up with more presence.

Quantum intention (crystal clear desire)

Plus

Newtonian intention (heart-centered next step)

Times

A high vibration (adequate sleep, nutrition, hydration, prayer, meditation, elevated emotion-feeling into the energy of the end result, *imagining it done*)

Over time (looking at it every day)

Equals

A flow state (a quantum leap)

As I mentioned in my first book, *Surf Your Pipe*, the clearer you are to a restaurant chef about how you prefer your meal, the more likely you are to get what you desire. And so, too, for all of our dreams, visions and goals.

TBH, I knew well that I felt stuck in the HIGH VIBRATION part of the equation.

— —— — —— —

I have seen something to be true. When we focus fully on ONE thing, with intention, we generally co-create that thing or something on a similar frequency. We amplify what we focus on.

I saw evidence of this when I recently attended the Onsite Healing Trauma workshop. All the facilitators came to the front of the room during the meet-and-greet. There was a line of about fifteen staff members, each standing next to the other. Each one was there to lead a group or an individual intensive program.

My eyes scanned the row and landed on a woman near the end. She had been the mentor in one of the groups I previously attended, and she was masterful in her work. I had already built-up trust with her, so if I were to be in her group again, that would give me a deeper foothold into showing up with more courage to do the inner work.

I KNEW I wanted to be in her group. I was so lit up to think there was a possibility that she would call me. I hoped and I wished, and I sent up a little prayer. I was so excited. I desired and longed to get called by her. My frequency was high. She was one of the last to call her group members. She called five out of six names. And then she paused.

"Chana?' she asked hesitantly, trying to pronounce the name.

Overcoming my shyness, I jumped forward. "Do you mean Chaya?" She laughed with me and said, "YES." What??!! I could have broken out into some dancing right there. I was in my groove. It felt like a life-gets-to-be-good vibe.

The following day a fellow was sitting in the auditorium with me, and we talked. He shared that when he saw all the therapists standing up front, there was just *one* he didn't have a good feeling about. He focused on the thought, anyone but that one...anyone but that one...anyone but that one...

And sure enough, THAT ONE called his name.

What a great example of how what we focus on expands.

We call towards us whatever we place our attention on. In my case, I focused on the person I desired as my group leader. In his case, he focused on who he didn't want. (He ended up moving past the resistance, connected with his mentor, and gained a lot!!) **We both got what we focused on.**

The subconscious mind is literal. It draws towards us whatever we choose to think about. The worries, problems, and anxieties, **or** how we would desire it all to be. The choice is in our hands.

You may ask, "Didn't they spend hours matching up therapists with participants? Didn't they make those decisions well before that meet and greet?"

True that, and yet aren't we operating on multi-dimensional, non-linear timelines in G-d's quantum field?

It was a cosmic rearranging.

'We are all creators of the illusory dimension of time.' (Duff Mc Donald in his book, *Tickled*)

— — — — —

I wrote this chapter wanting to uplevel. Well, I had to buckle up fast for the ride. G-d's universe showed me just where I was incongruent with what I thought I was ready for.

Generally, we come face to face with the part of our life where we have the most resistance to change, seemingly unrelated to the upgrade we thought we were looking for! (Thank you for that thought, Emily June Wilcox)

Here is how it all played out. I had set that intention to play bigger. To be "all in" for healing and to show up with more presence, impeccable with my word, as well as taking better care of my physical health to uplevel my frequency.

The next thing I knew, *I was down for the count.*

Things started shifting, and it was far from "pretty."

A situation showed up that was traumatizing (For details on that, you'll need to read my next book, the one under a pen name!)

I found myself knocked off of my feet. Victimized. (What!? I can't be here again!) After so much inner work. So much journaling, praying, walking, breathing, forgiveness exercises, boundary work, meditating, reading, and writing.

Had it all been for naught?

I knew better. I knew that I had the tools and resources to get unstuck, but who has that kind of emotional energy?

I understood that these feelings were all circling back around again because I was ready to process them deeper. (ugh) We subconsciously attract people and situations that put us face-to-face with our inner child's unmet emotional needs. Each person or situation that triggers us is the most current messenger of where we have something to process and heal.

It's an opportunity to take ownership of what we think, feel, need, and want. Once we acknowledge our actual emotional state, we can release whatever no longer serves us.

It was high time I self-sourced my internal validity so that I no longer would need to reenact situations that carried old wounds. (I know! I know! It's the journey of a lifetime, and there is always another level to process.)

When we can get off the merry-go-round of feeling "not good enough," our adult selves have the chance to meet our needs and we stop holding anyone else cosmically responsible for them. We are truly free when we do not need to 'take the bait' from someone else. Instead, we become present and let others own their issues. It's a graduation to emotional maturity when we can esteem ourselves appropriately (no one-upmanship nor putting ourselves down.) No more self-abandonment.

Brene Brown's classic share is that you can't selectively numb. So, if you are self-medicating your pain, shame, anger and grief, you are also numbing your feelings of joy and love.

I was not anticipating that when the date of my daughter Mia's first anniversary of passing went by, not only did my grief hit a 10/10, but unexpectedly, my anger came surging out of the woodwork and hit a 10/10. What?! I had done so much forgiveness work and processing. Was I still doing a spiritual bypass? How had I not realized I still carried so much anger inside me? Had it been leaking out sideways? I knew that repressed anger held a stress response that could affect one's physiology.

I was caught off guard.

Humbled.

I watched the feelings of anger, betrayal, injustice, and disappointment parade by. Instead of getting lost in them, I knew I had to FEEL and then DEAL. (Thanks for that tip, Zalman Nelson). It was time to take full responsibility for my emotional well-being. To tend to my old wounds. To wean myself off of needing external validation to feel whole. To self-partner.

I used all that rage to create a raging spiritual and emotional r/evolution for myself. I was invited to detach from some of my usual activities and more intimately focus on healing. It was back to the drawing board.

Out came the Melanie Tonia Evans 'quanta freedom' modules on taking back my personal power by taking responsibility to release any emotional charge showing up in my life. I knew that anywhere I held a lingering emotional charge to a certain feeling or negative experience, I could be magnetizing more of that toxic experience.

Out came the **All The Rage** masterclass I had taken with Melanie Ann Layer.

On went the Joe Dispenza YouTube videos about rewiring our neural pathways.

On went my headphones to listen to music as I allowed

the feelings to flood through my body as I power-walked the neighborhood.

Parallel to what I was experiencing, I watched one of my fave biz mentors, in real-time, navigate an intense emotional ride. Someone had been showing up with bullying energy online, setting off a critical mass of chaos. My mentor showed up humble, authentic, and raw, looking for anywhere possible to take accountability. I knew she would come through with her trademark dignity shining sacredly through her tears. It was messy as she tried to make heads or tails of the naysayer (in this case, hater) energy. The injustice was a travesty.

My worlds collided. Concurrent with my challenge, this mentor was dealing head-on with a high-conflict situation, modeling her humanity and leadership, holding onto her values and standards in the face of those with lowered communication standards. She created clearer boundaries around herself. It was art in the making.

I watched and calibrated. Legends are made in the way we choose to respond to our triggers. It's where our personal power can be up-leveled and leveraged.

It was a time and space for serious inner work. I didn't take it lightly. I did visualizations, read literature, journaled, and prayed as if my life depended on it. Because didn't it? What type of life is it to walk around victimized?

I wanted true freedom. Free to be the real me. Free to not take other people's drama personally. Free to protect myself with healthy boundaries, as needed, in the face of others (who weren't managing their feelings). People who are disconnected from their feelings can't fully honor someone else's.

I knew it was my responsibility to heal any subconscious trauma inside so that I would no longer need to experience it on the outside. I was determined to reset my nervous system.

I needed a new level of surrender to navigate my reality. The old template needed to be updated. I had outgrown the paradigm that had gotten me thus far. But, of course, nothing was moving the needle without a new level of surrender. Not a "giving up" type of surrender. The surrender into a deeper level of my more genuine self. A broader context of my life.

A putting of the inner critic to rest.

—----------

Months ago, while waiting in the security line at the LAX airport, I was surprised to see a sign that read:

No Threats

No Verbal Abuse

No Physical Violence of any kind

Fines up to $13,910.

The sign stopped me in my tracks, its bold words asserting the inherent worth of the transportation security officers. They were not available for abuse.

A pandemic of narcissism and high-conflict behavior attempts to stand in the way of our sovereignty. We can make a valiant effort to alchemize some of that to access our true soul worth. The 'dark triad' individuals (narcissists, sociopaths, and psychopaths) that manipulate without remorse (empathy-impaired per Lisa Romano) frequently bring people down so low that the ego goes offline, and the light goes back on in the soul. It's a homecoming.

There is a reckoning in the world at large inspired by an emerging, inner reckoning. People are finding their voice and speaking up against the violence playing out in the universe as they shake off trauma. The world is divinely transforming as individuals rise up and address their internal narcissist, the part inside of them that is self-critical and self-demeaning. Their ego defense mechanisms. The skeptic within. The attachment to an outdated narrative.

It's no coincidence that the possibility of sharing our voice with a reach of millions, by writing and easily self-publishing a book, is available and affordable for anyone and everyone. It is a key piece to this era of waking up to the deep voice inside that wants to be heard. I've heard it said that our voice is our healer.

I kept hearing my biz mentors talk about cleaning up any old energy of inadequacy by blessing and accepting all of ourselves, embracing our inherent wholeness, and rediscovering our soul potential.

I heard it and I heard it, and I heard it again but I had yet to embody it. And then, as I wrote this chapter and prayed for change to dissolve any old patterns or limiting beliefs keeping me feeling stuck and small, I came up against a reality that the previous level of me could not hold.

I needed a new context that was large enough to include this level of challenge. The feeling of victimization took hold of me emotionally, in its iron-like grip, and I couldn't find even momentary relief. Not even self-medicating with a sugar or Netflix binge could match this energy. It felt larger than me. I felt consumed with anger at an injustice playing out. There was no one outside of me that could make it go away. Once again, I was left with a cosmic meeting up with myself.

And in that sacred moment, as I showed up vulnerable and present in my pain, I ran into a more profound sense of self.

It was a billion-dollar feeling.

Having my own back.

Being worth my own time.

Being my own, honest-to-goodness, long-lost, best friend.

No one has walked my exact path.

No one can be there for me as well as me.

IF YOU FIGHT FOR YOUR LIMITATIONS, YOU GET TO KEEP THEM.

-JIM KWIK

The Wish List and a Straw Hat

There's a story of a king's son who went off to see the kingdom, armed with money for all his needs while traveling. Unfortunately, one thing led to another, and his money ran out. Over the next few years, things were so difficult for him that he slowly forgot that he had once been the king's very own son.

He worked manual labor jobs in the hot sun, trying to keep his body and soul together. Then, upon hearing that the King's chariot was slated to drive by his small town on its way back to the castle one fine day, the man penned a quick note and threw it into the royal wagon, as it sped by the town. He had practiced quite a few times to get the angle right to land his words through the small open carriage window, which was moving at lightning speed. The king reached down to read the note that had sailed in, amazed that someone had been successful in doing so.

It was a request for a straw hat.

The king recognized the royal handwriting of his son and cried bitter tears. He realized that his son had forgotten his origins and that his biggest ask was an inexpensive, relatively meaningless straw hat.

It's a metaphor for our soul that journeys into our body in this world, aspiring to weave together a connection between heaven and earth, spiritual and material.

Busy with the push and pull of everyday tasks, we often lose sight of the larger vision, focusing mainly on the 'straw hat' goals, requests, and desires on our wish list.

Sometimes, in the hitting up against spiritual/emotional checkpoints that temporarily destabilize us, we are reminded of who we really are and what we are here to do. We run into ourselves.

We are agents of change. We can change the way we see ourselves. We can change our thoughts. We can change our habits. When we interrupt the old patterns, we can soul-align with our **oneness** and reclaim our wholeness. It's our superpower.

In harnessing a redemptive mindset, armed with the embodiment of our inherent worth, we can **self-publish a book,** or **anything else** we set our mind to.

Whatever we believe is our limit, **is** our limit.

When I shared with my close friends and fam (the people who believe most in me) that I was writing and self-publishing a second book, they smiled kindly in understanding. They, for the most part (not all), held themselves back from gently explaining that a book wasn't a moneymaker. It was a therapeutic hobby in their eyes. I know they meant well and were just trying to "help me" be realistic. I appreciate it and know they had a good logical point.

I had to double down on my own belief that a book can be an aligned business move and a plentiful source of income, to avoid getting my energy pulled down by that, well-meaning, energy. I wired in Joe Dispenza's teaching that you have to amplify your desire higher than the circumstances in your environment to generate something new.

I'm the only one who needs to be sure. I can trust that it is safe to do things my way. To limit my time in conversations that drop my energy.

I take a lesson from Blackjack as a metaphor for discerning where to place my energy! When the card count is high, it's time to place a big bet to enhance your chance of winning, and when it's low, bet low enough just to stay in the game. I can apportion my precious energy in places where it is protected and amplified while wisely not squandering it with people or activities that lower my vibe.

It's our choice to be of high service to others by becoming the evidence for the next person, that it's possible to see your dream through.

Hey, if I can write and self-publish two books, even while mostly in survival mode, *anyone* can do it. TBH, I think the moments I was co-creating this book, are the moments that I was lifted way up into a state of flow. It's what got me jumping up early in the morning for the school carpool-run (with excitement despite my tiredness) as I would remember that I was in the throes of self-publishing a book about leveraging life's challenges to personally transform.

We intuit our desire. We decide it's possible. We move forward incrementally. And then, we do that again and again. It's creation at its finest when our work is aligned with our deepest self. It's soul work. As we heal and rediscover our true self, we free up energy and space to create. As we create, we further heal. It's an infinite loop of expansion. We become the embodiment of the highest truth of who we are. (Thank you for the activation of that concept for me, Dr. Andrea Morningstar. As we create, so we are created, and as we are created, so we create...)

When we desire to bring our voice back online from whatever state of numbness (unconsciousness) we find ourselves in, writing is one of many therapeutic tools that help dissolve stress and replenish energy. (Per Steven Kotler; on leveraging creativity and curiosity to embody mindfulness and find your flow state.)

It's time to rewrite the code. Rewire our neural pathways. Break the mold. Answer the call. Break new ground. Create a new level of freedom. We decide the time is right now. We open our heart. We go all in. We learn to counteract our limiting beliefs by trusting that we can stay present, no matter what. Even in disappointment. We move past the fear of "what if this doesn't work?"

The environment raises to meet our energy. We start compounding our energy and momentum. No longer stuck on a linear pathway. (Thanks for the inspiration, Genevieve

Rackham)

All roads lead us home to our most authentic selves.

Redemption begets redemption.

WHATEVER THE MIND CAN CONCEIVE AND BELIEVE, IT CAN ACHIEVE.

-NAPOLEAN HILL

Surf Your Pipe Squared

At some point, I had to filter out just about all of the voices and to-dos in my external environment and actively direct my adrenaline and energy inwards to self-publish. Even as good ideas came in (for example, my brother Ben recommending that I get a well-known person to write a PRAISE FOR the book), I had a deep sense that I was working with a delicate window of momentum to submit the manuscript as it was. It was a 'done is better than perfect' moment. I didn't want my energy to stall.

Anything else would have to be for a second edition or a second book, otherwise, it could derail the process of hitting the submit button. I could still be working on my first book if I hadn't held my energy stable and solid behind the decision to push past any resistance and SELF-PUBLISH **NO MATTER WHAT.**

It's the moment when your book morphs from hobby and side note to your business. It becomes *The ONE Thing* (per Gary Keller and Jay Papasan) that is your primary focus. It's the moment you live at the outer limits of achievement to produce extraordinary results. You live big and take a leap of faith. That's where the magic happens. You temporarily limit some access of time and energy for other people and things. You purposefully block out time.

Your book becomes the G. One of my daughters lovingly and playfully says, "Ma, you're the G" whenever I drive her over the canyon to her hip-hop dance class. I finally asked what that meant. (It seemed to have a positive connotation!) She said it was short for the Greatest of All Time.)

I had no idea that self-publishing itself would open the door to a second book, and isn't that the best evidence of how it all adds up? Even doing something imperfectly takes us right to our next opportunity.

During the final week of uploading all of the elements of my book, there were a couple of days of calls to KDP to ask questions regarding the best way to submit it. At that point, I had some essentials packed into my handbag (headphones, phone charger, snacks, felt tip pens). I had situated myself at a local Starbucks, knowing that I needed to give this my complete focus, without the kids bursting into my room asking what there was to eat! (My youngest being 15 years old.)

KDP was good about returning my calls when I sent a request in. They were generous with their time.

As I wrote this chapter, I searched up the 2023 iconic surfing event Billabong Pipeline Masters, the "holy grail" of surf, to remind myself of how I got my inspiration for the title of my first book—*Surf Your Pipe*— a metaphor I found helpful in navigating life.

January 29- February 10, 2023

Just 48 days, 8 hours, 46 min, and 7 seconds away.

Bonzai Pipeline, North Shore, Oahu, Hawaii, United States.

The most globally watched surf event in the world.

On a deep level, the surfers were competing against themselves as they barrelled through massive Pacific swells and a shallow reef. It was not for amateurs.

My life felt like quite the advanced adventure as I was swept into tackling rough wipeouts between the wave windows.

A state of being so intense and exquisite that I was invited to reimagine my very being, drive more creativity, and harness the momentum of the 'back-door waves.'

What **was** the mindset held by Kelly Slater, Jack Robinson, Carissa Moore, John John Florence, Italo Ferreira, and Gabriel Medina as they detached from the buzz on the beach and **sought redemption**? Despite the risks, they were searching for surfing's ultimate ride, where one can be anything but afraid.

In this new era, they were less defined by the wins and losses of their professional career, and more by their timeless adrenaline, their 'punch through the curtain' to get a completion, and their courage to set aside fear in their quest. They were poised and relaxed, comfortable as they held a solid momentum, flying through their section with dynamic, high-speed turns, 'stable on the foam ball and zipping out the bottom'.

They rebirthed in the epicenter of each wave, and champions were made.

Lives were changed in the decision of a moment, to commit to the wave or not, with energy second to none. Their single most significant achievement less about the hype of a perfect ten with its accolades and more about the personal growth in **a state of flow.**

A pinnacle of personal redemption.

No holds barred.

The surfer is invited to take his attention off the external conditions of his life so that he can be fully present at the moment. Nothing less will suffice.

In a day and age where $16 trillion is projected to be spent annually on mental health, accessing one's inner state is a serious business. Our soul is pinging us as we walk our path, hoping we will feel worth our own time and take a moment to meet up with ourselves.

We have the power to heal our inner emotional pain.

Our healing is our responsibility.

We can break free of any trauma reality.

We may have been traumatized by other people acting out their unconscious trauma programming.

We can't fix, control, or change anyone else.

We can find resolution within.

We change our reality on the inside, and the outside follows.

We can wake up to a new perception.

We can choose a broader context.

We can shift out of a victim-consciousness.

We can stop holding other people responsible for our energy.

We shift from blame to personal responsibility.

We choose an up-leveled emotional resonance.

The consciousness we hold makes all of the difference.

The Real Questions

Deep questions are a shortcut to the subconscious mind, which drives most of our habits and behaviors.

To recondition the default thoughts in my subconscious mind, I ask myself the most profound questions I can contemplate, so as to gain conscious access. It's a hack to access the part of my mind where I can influence and rewire neural pathways to the upgraded belief systems I'd like to embody.

What fuels my creative fire?

____

____

What's my innovative edge?

____

____

How can I be more of the real me?

____

____

What else is possible?

____

____

How does it get better than this?

What if today was THE day?

How can my book change lives?

What's my definition of success?

Is it current?

Does it inspire?

What is my purpose?

How do I get an awareness of my purpose?

What one small, heart-centered action am I ready to take?

What's the ONE thing I could do today that will be most significant in my big pic?

What would I do if I couldn't be judged?

Would I do this for no money?

Am I attached to an outdated narrative?

Am I honoring and tending to my inner wounds?

What thoughts align me?

____

____

What beliefs serve me?

____

____

How do I handle difficulty?

____

____

Where am I in resistance to my current reality?

____

____

Where am I welcome to be myself?

____

____

How do I handle making a 'mistake'?

____

____

Is my vibe contingent on a 'good' or 'bad' day?

____

____

When I look back, how do I want to remember this time?

____

____

Am I overlooking my life as it happens?

____

____

Am I offering assistance to others uninvited?

____

____

How do I lead myself through difficult things?

____

____

Am I treating my soul purpose like a side note?

____

____

How do I measure success?

____

____

Do I leave enough space to take care of myself?

____

What are my emotional coordinates? What do I think about me? Do I get me?

Can I hold space for me?

How much do I worry about what others think of me?

Am I continually upleveling my emotional recovery? (Elevating my consciousness)

What's the best version of myself that I can be in this moment?

What energy am I choosing to compound?

Who am I holding responsible for my problems?

B"H

Self-Publishing Affirmations

Connect with the heart of who you are.

Connect with the shared heart of humanity.

Tune it to what makes you feel alive and joyous.

Your purpose is bigger than you. It belongs to the whole world.

Prayers and conversations help.

Your purpose is your inheritance. You don't have to pay for it.

Money can't buy it.

Redefine success.

Life is calling us to heal and be present.

Alignment is my superpower.

When I vibrate in fear, it evokes fear in other people.

It's ok to be imperfect. It's our humanity.

What should have been safe for us may not have been.

There's no there. We are here.

We realize we are enough—no need to internalize our value by how people treat us.

When we aren't conscious, we project things onto others.

Instead of "why did you do that?" we can ask, "Can you help me understand what was going on for you?"

We are what we practice.

Wholeness is found in the yearning for it.

No need to destroy the old to build the new.

Growth and perpetual movement are dynamics of the soul.

I trust myself.

I create my legacy.

I'm here to be of service.

I get to change lives.

I know who I am.

I go all in.

I rise.

I take me with me.

I am worth my own time.

It's all adding up.

I'm willing to meet my own emotional needs.

It starts with me.

Everything in my life has the possibility to expand me.

I honor the process.

I can't buy my way into who I want to be.

I can embody it and be it.

I liberate myself from trauma.

I envision what is possible.

I integrate the past with the present moment.

I stay the course.

Inspired by: Robert Holden, Melanie Ann Layer, Genevieve Rackham, Amanda Frances, Cara Alwil, Melanie Tonia Evans, Joe Dispenza, and the Onsite Healing Trauma workshop.

THOUGHT IS POTENT

-YOSEF YITZCHAK SCHNEERSON

92

Conclusion

We have the capacity to **illuminate** our environment. A book is one way to do so. As with everything, when we set an intention and make a decision to move ahead on our vision, our micro step forward will draw our goal towards us with a magnetic energy. Whatever genre your book, the sacred gift of your essence is shared to the collective.

I'm not sure why in some areas of life I find it easier to show up than others. It's likely my gut and intuition directing and defining my vision, having more info than my conscious self does. I think that as we collect evidence that we can see our dreams through in one area, we open ourselves up to the belief of more possibility in other areas. It's the journey of a lifetime.

They say strategy isn't everything. While I like a to-do list to remind me of my focus and priorities on the daily, it's 'frequency first' that will animate a flow state. When I'm in my feminine energy, fully alive and awake, I set in motion a 'domino effect' momentum that propels my strategy forward with a quantum leap.

My thoughts today are creating my tomorrow.

When I'm conscious and fully present, in a consistent way, my imagination and emotion (feeling into the end result I desire) become my inner programming. My inner dialogue is powerful. When I see and bemoan the lack in any situation, I manifest more lack. Lack begets lack.

When I perceive and receive the abundance already available in every moment, more abundance manifests in physical form. Abundance begets abundance.

It's not that I don't address the true feelings of my reality. It's that I also seek out evidence of the actual blessings, growth, and gifts **already** there. I raise my frequency by making the subconscious conscious. I unpack anything blocking my willingness and readiness to internalize a higher reality. I integrate all parts of myself.

I pave a new pathway with higher possibilities.

I up my emotional intelligence so I can self-regulate with self-ownership, listening for my soul's whisper. (Thanks, Ani Lipitz)

When I get in touch with the personal redemption in any area of my life, (anywhere I have shifted and transformed from a victim mindset to one of empowerment) I solidify and reinforce that energy. Redemption begets redemption.

It's a choice. I am in control of my headspace and my vibration. I take responsibility to work on my thinking, personal growth, and well-being.

Intentionally choosing the mindset, energy, and strategy behind whatever I decide to do is the determining factor of the outcome. We are blessed with the power to take huge jumps in our personal effectiveness when we align with our true divine calling.

It's my hope that this short self-publishing "primer" act

as a muse to activate your own self-publishing vision, or whatever your heart desires, in the way of a quantum-leap!

Final Thought

Self-publishing the second time around was EASY AS PIE. Seriously. Minus the anxiety (of the first time) at bumping up against unknown processes, there was a gentle rhythm to it. For example, I easily paid with a cc for the ISBN and bar code on Bowker. (No inner drama necessary this time.) I then circled back to my Bowker account to assign my title, tagline, and book description. I knew to screenshot/ save it so that it would be handy when I uploaded the manuscript to Amazon's KDP. No last-minute scramble for that info this time.

I breezed through the categories in under an hour. KDP said the book cover needed an imprint. I vaguely remembered that from the first time. I think it meant my name since I was self-publishing. I added it. No biggie.

As I've been getting closer to self-publishing this second book, I'm hearing some friends wistfully share that they desire to write their book but feel stuck. They aren't sure where to start. They aren't sure how to safely write about other people, who were part of their experience, without being sued. They don't feel tech-savvy and therefore feel stalled from opening a Google doc.

While all of those things are important to address, I'm starting to see how it's our ***decision*** to own the thought and belief that it's POSSIBLE. It's our choice in hitting any goal. As much as I can help them address their concerns (try voice notes if you don't like writing...start with a notepad if technology gives you anxiety…begin with whichever piece of the story calls to you and free-write and then decide how to edit names for privacy), it's their **thinking** holding them back more than their circumstance.

I saw that to be true for myself a few months ago when I was debating whether to exhibit my authentic mini tambourine keychains at a trade show in New York in Feb 2023. I didn't have the funds available to stock my product or pay for the booth and accessories (gift bags, business cards, etc.)

Not only that, but a dark cloud was upon me as Nov 2022 came around, marking the one-year date since my daughter Mia's passing. A profound loneliness had set in, leaving me emotionally in a tight, constricted place.

I needed an infusion of soulfulness, light, and joy. A deeper awareness of how to interpret my reality. A grounding. A coherence.

I could have easily reasoned that I was stuck, emotionally and financially, and I would have been correct.

I knew deep down that there is a quantum opening when we draw upon the infinite resource of our divine essence. The gift from our Creator. I was grounded in that truth. Taking a bite of my flaky mushroom quiche with a swig of latte, I made a decision to do everything in my personal power to make it happen, unattached to the actual outcome.

The situation called for a boss move. I'd need to place the order for production on my product within a day or two, for it to be delivered in time, as well as book the spot at the show. I leveraged the resources already there (waiting behind the curtain for my readiness) by reaching out to three customers who I knew were considering placing an order but had hesitated. (One potential new one and two existing ones).

I met them where they were at. I offered the new one a lower MOQ (min order quantity) and free shipping. They were in.

I offered one existing customer the lower price point she had been pressing for on a large order. Honestly, it left me with barely any margin of profit, but having the cash flow on that day was of high service and value to me and my plan. The third customer had been hoping to place a large order but didn't have the funds. I encouraged her to place a smaller order that was more affordable and offered to throw in some free product. It came together with relative ease. It was a win-win-win. My customers were happy, and I was able to place my order in a timely way. As G-d's universe conspires to mirror our efforts, a friend reached out and offered to lend me the $500 to book the table, and two other people generously offered to sponsor the extras to enhance the booth.

The energy at the event was off the charts. The results were greater than I even anticipated. Evidence that it's our intentional thinking and heart-felt decision that sets in motion the momentum to catch a wave/a flow state towards our vision and dream. Changing the energy around a 'stuck' thought is a jedi move.

It's been a privilege sharing the ins and outs with the emerging author in you. Your soul's inner self-expression is online. Lead with your legacy, it's unlike any other. You can't be replicated.

Time to play full-out and self-publish! When that bulky, brown package (carrying your newly launched book), lands with a thud at your front doorstep, it really hits.

B"H

Thank You's

I asked my father which part of my first book he most related to, and his answer was the **Acknowledgments** section. (Wait, was that his way of saying he didn't love the book? Or was he leading with a legacy of gratitude?!)

Thank you to my good friend Dalia, who saw me free-falling and said, "Let's go take care of *the thing*," thereby restoring my faith in the goodness of humanity. You organically champion the dignity and rights of women. It's a calling. May your family be redemptively blessed in a way of malchus.

Thank you to my sis Abby, the light of my life. Thanks for your steadfastness and incredible outpouring of love. We are traversing this life-time side by side—every blessing for ease and support on you and your fam's soul's journey.

Thank you to my sis Tzip. I am humbled by your emotional maturity, sensitivity, wisdom, and kindness. May your blessings overflow. Thanks for the Target orders, the reality checks, and the gift of you. Xoxo Tambourine on!

Thank you to my brother Ben. You model leadership, taking on the role of 'older brother' even though you are younger, adding immeasurable support. You have a way of laughing at life's challenges and letting them slide off graciously. May your family be supported immeasurably, and may you truly enjoy your celebrations on a deep level, physically, emotionally, materially, and spiritually!

Thank you to my brother Aaron for your dry humor, friendship, support, and being a model of humility, integrity, and equanimity. May your family's blessings spread wide and far and deep.

Thank you to my brother Zevy for organizing all that learning in Mia's honor and for showing up in the most important moments. I have no words. May you and your beautiful fam be blessed spiritually and materially. You are wise beyond your years and lead with your caring heart.

Thank you, Bubby and Zeidushka, for the legacy of trusting in G-d's goodness. That charge has carried me through the darkest nights. May you be strengthened physically, emotionally, spiritually, and financially. May you celebrate many joyous occasions with good health and inner peace.

Thank you, Yael, for believing in me and the tambourine biz. Your generosity of spirit inspires me. May you be blessed to be a great giver and lender. May you heal for real. May your blessings overflow. May you experience deep peace of mind.

Thank you, Joanne Kipust Siegel, for the generous offer to edit this manuscript. I loved the comments! So happy that we reconnected over Facebook and coffee dates at the bagel shop. May you and your fam be blessed with tranquility and an overflow of revealed blessings.

Thank you Sylky Resnicoff for holding space.

Thank you Zalman Nelson for reminding me to tend to my own thoughts and feelings.

Thank you, Faye, and Eti for having my back at Mia's funeral and always.

Thank you, Becky, for the charge to imagine it done. Every blessing to you.

Thank you, Goldie, for the mutual mentorship. Your depth and desire for personal growth inspire me.

Thank you, Odeya, for your friendship and the coffee dates.

Thank you, Aliza Marton. You are the queen of lifting the next woman up, anywhere you can. Every blessing!

To my Creator

Thank you for bringing my kids and I to this day. For standing us up on firm ground. For safeguarding us and overflowing our blessings. For each corner we have turned. Please bless us to heal for real, to tap into our inherent wholeness, and be guided forward in the most optimal way possible on our Divine journeys. May we rise up and add support to the unfolding redemptive consciousness in the world and co-create the most extraordinary love story ever...

A harmony between all of humanity and our Creator

XOXO

Chaya Mechal hzg

To my mentors, my fam, my friends, my readers, my collective sisters,

Thanks for being exactly who you are, where you are.

Let's do this 'personal redemption' thing.

Let's find our way together. Let's lift ourselves and each other up.

What else is there?

Chaya Mechal Holland hzg

Xoxo

Tambourinegirl_tofmiriam.biz (Instagram)

Chaya Mechal Holland Hzg (Facebook)

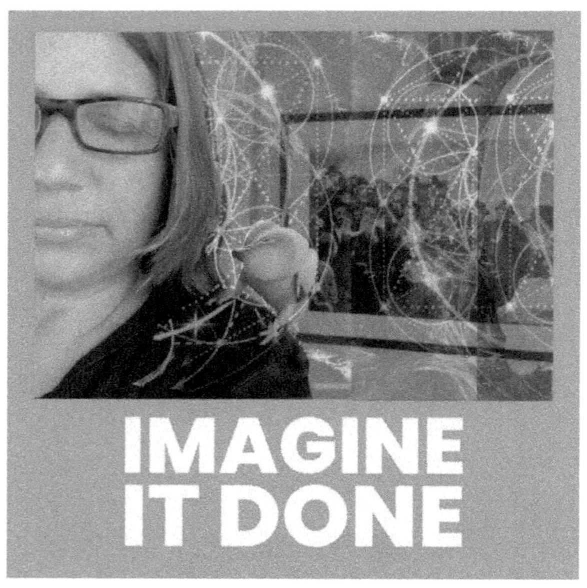

THIS BOOK IS DEDICATED TO:

SRULI & MUSSI
SAM
KIRA
MIA (a"h)
BRACHA
BETZALEL
PENINA

THANK YOU FOR INVITING ME TO UPLEVEL MY EQ
EVERY SINGLE DAY. MAY YOU BE BLESSED!

XOXO IMA, MAMA, MA, MOM

B"H

B"H

B"H

B"H